Creative Characters

A Quick Guide to Writing Well

P.S. Wells

Pegwood Publishing

Title: How to Craft Creative Characters

By P.S. Wells

Subjects: 1. Authorship Reference (Books)

2. Writing Skill Reference (Books)

3. Creativity (Books)

Key Words: How to write, character, character-driven story, creativity, fiction writing, write story, write fiction

ISBN ebook: 979-8-9879809-8-9

ISBN paperback: 979-8-9879809-9-6

Published by Pegwood Publishing

Roanoke IN 46783

Contents

Chapter One

On Your Mark, Get Set, Write

B efore you begin writing, save time and effort by knowing these four things.

1. What is your idea?

2. Who is your audience?

3. How does your idea, message, or story benefit your audience?

4. What is the best method to share your idea to your particular audience?

Every project begins with an idea.

First, decide what is the story or message, lesson or insight you want to share?

Hone the idea down to a laser point. The tighter the focus the better you stay on target. The tighter the message the easier for your reader to follow where you take them.

Do not be intimidated to find others have written on the same topic. You have your own slant, your own experience, your own insight which is unique to you. There is always room in the market for fresh ways of thinking on a familiar topic. Your voice will be different from other authors.

Put considerable thought into how you will present your idea in a unique fashion.

What is your idea?

Second, you have an idea, message, or story you want to share. The question is, who do you want to share your message with?

Before you begin, clarify exactly who you are speaking to. This is as important as dialing a specific number when you make a phone call.

No project – outside God's Word – is for everyone. Who is your target audience? Who is interested in receiving your message?

Age, education level, ethnicity, faith, gender, hobbies, interests, and profession are among the considerations when you define your audience. Academics, artists, and athletes each have unique jargon and terminology as do zoning specialists, zoologists, and zoo keepers. Bestselling author, Jerry Jenkins, pictured his mother sitting across the desk as he wrote his novels. She represented the audience he had in mind for the stories he told.

How specific can you be when you describe your audience?

· *The Ten Best Decisions A Single Mom Can Make* is practical help and tangible tips for solo parents ages 24 to 45, eager to create a healthy and successful family.

· *Slavery in the Land of the Free* informs intermediate and high school students about human trafficking in the United States.

· Geared for four to eight-year-olds, *The Girl Who Wore Freedom* is the true story of five-year-old Dany who was given Lifesavers and liberty on D-Day.

Writing to children is completely different from communicating with teens which differs from sharing with adults. Generally speaking, the vocabulary that appeals to women is not the same as the descriptions that resonate with men. While the words in a toddler's board book are chosen as carefully as the text for a novel, the volume is exceedingly fewer. Knowing your audience guides your vocabulary level and the length of your project in the same way you craft a conversation with an industry professional far differently than you prepare to talk with a child.

Third, how does your idea, message, or story benefit your audience? Why would your reader trade their hard-earned funds to purchase your project? Why would someone invest their limited time to read your writing?

In other words, what take-home value do you provide?

Types of take-home value writers offer include

- entertainment

- education

- guidance

- humor

- how-to instruction

- inspiration

- information

When you pen a project to be viewed and consumed by others, you create an exchange. You expect your audience to read your writing. Your audience expects you will make the experience of reading your work worthwhile. To keep your end of the agreement, clarify the benefit you plan to provide. Purposefully and generously give your audience abundant take-home value.

Fourth, once you know your audience and the take-home value you will provide to that audience, it's time to decide on the best vehicle to convey your message. There are myriad ways for a writer to communicate including

apps
articles
books
children's books
curriculum
greeting cards
novel
screenplay

song

web content

As writers, we have myriad formats to connect with readers. When you know your target audience, and the take-home value you want to deliver, then consider what format will be the most effective to share your message. You have plenty of options.

A writer has one job to do and that is to elicit an emotional response in the reader. When you write a book or want to improve a story, how can you use character to elicit emotion within your reader?

Creative characters are the ones that live in the reader's mind beyond the final page of a story.

At its core, character is the organization and structure of a person's character or personality.

Chapter Two

Character Is

You have a story to share, a message to tell through writing. There are foundational aspects to writing well including well-crafted characters.

Essentials for a powerful story are

1. a character the reader cares about

2. a very great life-changing, world-impacting need the character must achieve

3. a great obstacle between the character we care about and the character's life-changing, world-impacting need

Critical elements for a compelling, memorable story that works include

- Pivotal Plots

- Memorable Characters

- Sensational Settings

- Dynamic Dialog

- Point of View

Character is the organization and structure of a person's character or personality.

What is the difference between a character and a character we care about? Consider your favorite books and films. Most likely, that story lingers in your memory because you became emotionally invested.

Recall a book you set aside before finishing. Or a film that you won't waste time or money watching again. Typically, these characters were two-dimensional rather than three-dimensional. We may stay with the story to see what happens but not because the ending matters personally.

Connecting with a story is subjective. My daughter liked *The Croods* film, but I didn't see the charm. I saw the first (now the fourth) *Star Wars* movie eleven times in the theater although she can't understand why. A book becomes a New York Times bestseller, and a film becomes a blockbuster when a lot of people care about a character and what happens to that character.

Part of what makes an audience interested is the character's great need. While needing to pass a school spelling test is not compelling, needing to traverse impossible terrain in the worst weather to bring home medicine that will save the lives of those you love is gripping.

- Will the character succeed?

- If I were in that setting, would I have the courage to try?

- When the character is terrified, will he continue on the journey?

- When the character has the opportunity to quit, will she?

- How will the character respond to life-threatening danger?

- What if the character fails?

In January 1925, the Alaskan city of Nome experienced a deadly outbreak of diphtheria. Thousands would die without the antitoxin serum. Twenty dog mushers banded together to bring the life-saving medicine hundreds of miles across frozen terrain from Anchorage in just 127 hours to save the people of the city. These brave people are remembered in the yearly Iditarod challenge.

Consider the main characters and the sidekicks in these highest-grossing films.

#1 *Gone With the Wind* 1939 (Adjusted for inflation)
#2 *Avengers Endgame* 2019
#3 *Avatar* 2009
#4 *Titanic* 1977
#5 *Star Wars, The Force Awakens* 2015

- Why do audiences care about what happens to these characters?

- What characteristics are endearing?

- In what ways does the character's challenges seem relevant to your own experience?

- Is the character perfect?

- How does the obstacle between the character and the character's great need bring out the best in the character?

- How does the obstacle bring out the character's worst?

- How does the character change?

- How is the character's actions similar to what you would do in a similar situation?

- How is the character's reactions completely different from how you would respond?

- What do you learn about yourself by observing the character?

- How do you identify with the character's heroic journey?

Use these questions to explore how to create your own character that your audience cares about. Initially, the audience doesn't have to like a character. No one likes Scrooge in the opening of *A Christmas Carol*. Yet, as an audience, we are willing to go along on the journey with the old curmudgeon.

Though completely fictional, Scrooge is so iconic that people who have not read the book by Charles Dickens still know what is meant when someone is described as being a Scrooge.

Charles Dickens created a classic character that audiences have cared about for generations. A character the audience cares about is the first essential ingredient for your memorable story.

Chapter Three

What Does Your Character Want?

T hree essentials are common to every compelling story.

•An interesting character the audience cares about

• The character's great need

• An insurmountable obstacle between the character and the great need the character must achieve

Having created a winsome character, what is the character's great need?

According to Maslow's Hierarchy of Need, humans require

• food and clothing

• safety

• love and belonging

- esteem

- self-actualization

An absence or scarcity in these areas automatically creates a powerful need for our character.

For instance, in Andy Weir's novel, *The Martian*, the main character is stranded alone on the planet Mars where he quickly realizes he needs the life-sustaining elements of oxygen, warmth, food, and shelter. These needs are compounded by the additional requirements for safety and relationship.

In Lin-Manuel Miranda's *Hamilton*, the young orphan learns how to get the basics of food, clothing, and shelter. Spurred by his upbringing, he longs for love and belonging, esteem and self-actualization. While many wish to avoid war, Hamilton sees the Revolutionary War as his opportunity to prove himself and make a name.

To create a great need for your character we care about:

1. Threaten your character's basic needs, the ones that support existence.

2. Complicate their physical needs with longings of the heart including acceptance, belonging, connection, relationship, and love.

3. Limit the character's amount of time to achieve their big need.

4. To broaden the scope, set up the character's big need to

impact not only the character, but others of importance to the character.

- How are others impacted when the character achieves his big need?

- Who is harmed if the character achieves their big need?

- Who is hurt if the character fails?

- What choice does the character make when his deepest desire is at odds with the greater good?

For instance, will Captain America choose true love with Peggy or save New York City from nuclear destruction? What does Peggy want him to do? If he chooses love, could that love be enjoyed—or even survive, in the wake of the destruction of so many people? If he saves New York, will that cost his life? Does Captain America truly have a choice in this setting?

Keep your reader turning pages to follow a memorable character striving to grasp a great need.

- Multiply tension by setting Grand Canyon-sized obstacles between the character and the character's deep need.

- Give your reader reason to believe reaching their desired goal will exact a huge cost.

- Provide reason for the reader to suspect the character will not achieve their great need at all.

- Alert your reader that what the character thinks he needs may not be what he really needs.

In the creation of your story, introduce the character, and quickly establish the character's vital need. How can you complicate the need, fill the path with obstacles on the way to achieve the need, and what will be the result of accomplishing the goal?

Chapter Four

The Main Characteristics About Main Characters

S tories are plot-driven or character-driven, and even better when you create a story that is plot- and character-driven.

Plot is what people do and why they do it. Character is the internal organization and structure of a person that motivates how the character responds to external pressures. In story, the writer places a specific personality into a specific setting and the reader follows as the character reacts and responds.

Generally, the principle players in a story consist of

- Main character

- Sidekick

- Antagonist

- Mentor

Consider your audience as you assemble a main character. When writing about a real person, see that person through the eyes of your reader. What is your reader's age, education level, faith, gender, and interests?

- Male readers tend to prefer to read about a male protagonist

- Female readers generally are happy to read about a male or female protagonist

- Female protagonists tend to have a larger female audience

- Youth are eager to be older and read about older characters who are in the next stage of life. For instance, middle schoolers want to read about those in high school.

Will your main character be human or animal? E. B. White made a writing career with main characters from the animal kingdom including the spider Charlotte Cavatica of *Charlotte's Web*, a mouse named Stuart in *Stuart Little*, and Louis the swan in *Trumpet of the Swan*.

Popular main characters who are animals include

- Bambi in *Bambi*

- Fiver and Hazel, rabbits in *Watership Down*

- Hank in the *Hank the Cowdog* series

- Mrs. Frisbee in *Mrs. Frisbee and the Rats of NIMH*, Peter of *Peter Rabbit*

- Simba of *Lion King*

- Winnie the Pooh in the *Winnie the Pooh* series

Human main characters come in all ages and from everywhere on the globe.

- Laura Ingalls Wilder in the *Little House on the Prairie* series

- Jean Valjean in *Les Miserables*

- Scarlet O'Hara in *Gone With the Wind*

- Tom Sawyer in *Tom Sawyer*

- Scrooge in *A Christmas Carol*

- Wang Lung in *The Good Earth*

- Jean Louise 'Scout' Finch in *To Kill A Mockingbird*

Some protagonists are from different worlds of the author's imagination.

- Katniss Everdeen in the *Hunger Games*

- Frodo Baggins in *Lord of the Rings*

- Meg Murry in *A Wrinkle in Time*

- Lucy Pevensiein *The Lion, The Witch, and the Wardrobe*

- Tris Prior of the *Divergent* series

Main characters who live in our memories and in popular culture long after we finish reading the book are relatable to the reader. They are not perfect but share characteristics that mirror our own.

Far from flawless, Harry Potter was relatable to readers. He was
- a young hero

- scholarly looking in his glasses

- filled with curiosity

- experienced real emotions

- had solemn intelligence

- delighted in discovery

- longed deeply for family

What is your character good at? Kya Clark of *Where The Crawdads Sing* by Delia Owens is skilled at observing nature. This ability becomes her way to support herself. Percy Blakeney in *Scarlet*

Pimpernel is a natural actor, a strength that allows him to save lives. Eugenia 'Skeeter' Phelan in *The Help* employs her stubborn sense of justice to confront social norms.

What is your character most afraid of? What is your character's kryptonite? For Mallory Wayne in *The Patent*, she fears looking incompetent and losing her last family member. In *The Last Letter From Your Lover* by Jojo Moyes, Jennifer Stirling is afraid to be treated as an outcast by family and friends. A character's fears are core to how your character acts. Those fears are also a relatable touchpoint with your reader.

What is unique about your main character? While all people look fairly alike having a head and shoulders, knees and toes, describe the traits that set your character apart. Clive Cussler's Dirk Pitt has aquamarine eyes. Mr. Dodson in Melanie Benjamin's *Alice I Have Been* has one eye higher than the other. Sherlock Holmes is socially inept and quirky.

Does he wear a ponytail and ride his bike to work like patent attorney Marc Wayne in *The Patent?* Does he have hands ragged and scarred with black nails and a sabre cut across his cheek like Captain Long John Silver in *Treasure Island?* Can she slide up the staircase banister like Mary Poppins?

When creating your main character, whether the character is real or made-up, ask yourself these questions.

- Who is your audience?

- Is your character animal or human?

- What is your character good at?

- What is your character afraid of?

- What relatable traits does your character have?

- What unique characteristics does your character have?

Chapter Five

The Best Side of Sidekicks

I n story, the author places personalities into specific settings and the reader follows as the collection of characters reacts and responds. Generally, the principle players in a story consist of

- Main character

- Sidekick

- Antagonist

- Mentor

Sidekicks fill important roles as close companion, partner, friend, or travel buddy to the main character.

Consider your audience as you assemble a sidekick. If your protagonist is male, a female companion can broaden your audience.

When the main character is female, a male sidekick can expand the story's appeal, though a female hero with a male sidekick is rare.

- Margaret Houlihan to Hawkeye Pierce in *M.A.S.H.*

- Tinkerbell to Peter Pan

Will your sidekick be human or animal or something different? In the *Peanuts* cartoons, Snoopy is a dog with a bird named Woodstock for a sidekick.

- Groot to Rocket Racoon in Guardians of the Galaxy

- Mushu, the family's guardian dragon faithfully accompanies Mulan.

- Olaf is the friendly and extroverted snowman to reserved Elsa and Anna in *Frozen*.

From the first *Star Wars* film, R2-D2 bravely faces every challenge to champion the good guys from Padme and Anakin to Leia, Luke, Obi-Wan and Han Solo. The winsome Artoo is particularly trustworthy because as a robot, the silver and blue sidekick has no personal agenda.

While Han Solo serves as sidekick to Luke Skywalker, Chewbacca is Han Solo's wingman. A sidekick with a sidekick.

Notable sidekicks include
- Becky Thatcher and Huckleberry Finn to Tom Sawyer

- Bucky Barnes to Captain America

- Doc Brown to Marty McFly in *Back to the Future*

- Drover to Hank in *Hank the Cowdog*

- Ethel Mertz to Lucille Ball in *I Love Lucy*

- Friday to Robinson Crusoe

- Hermione Granger and Ron Weasley to Harry Potter in the *Harry Potter* series

- Jeeves in *My Man Jeeves*

- Jiminy Cricket to Pinocchio

- Nick "Goose" Bradshaw to Pete Maverick Mitchell in *Top Gun*

- Pacha to Kuzco in *Emperor's New Groove*

- Pancho to the Cisco Kid

- Sebastian to Ariel in *Little Mermaid*

A great sidekick is a complex character who
- completes the hero's set of skills.

Tonto's unique abilities include survival skills outside city limits for Ranger John Reid in *The Lone Ranger.*
- provides contrast to the hero's style.

Spock is logic and social commentary to the emotional and contradictory humanness of Captain James T. Kirk of *Star Trek.*
- balances the main character's personality.

Dr. John Watson bridges Sherlock Holmes' lack of social skills with the eccentric detective's usefully keen intellect.
- adds humor.

Al Giordino provides mechanical know-how and comedic relief in Clive Cussler's Dirk Pitt series.
- often inadvertently provides the solution.

Gromit never speaks – in fact the faithful pooch doesn't have a mouth – yet Gromit resourcefully rescues Wallace from his misbehaving inventions in the *Wallace and Gromit* stop-motion comedy animation.
- has the best dialog lines.

Who else could pull off phrases like "Holy Uncanny Photographic Mental Processes," "Holy Priceless Collection of Etruscan Snoods," or "Holy Astringent Plum-Like Fruit" except Burt Ward as Robin to Adam West's Batman?
- is loyal.

Sancho Panza's name is synonymous with sidekick as an example of loyalty to Don Quixote.

- personifies the story's theme.

No matter the danger, Samwise Gamgee won't let Frodo lose his way geographically or spiritually on his all-consuming trek to save Middle-earth. At Frodo's breaking point, Sam pledges that while he cannot carry his master's burden, "but I can carry you."

In my adventure novel, *Chasing Sunrise*, Michael Northington is the main character while Bryce Lassiter is the sidekick. Bryce's easy-going nature softens Michael's seriousness, Bryce has the fun dialog lines, and this battle buddy's intuitive skills pave the way for Michael to be the hero.

Their history together has created a friendship where each intuitively knows what the other needs. In the Philippines, Michael encounters a young girl on the brink of a lifestyle that will destroy her life.

Standing beside Michael, Bryce stuffed his hands in his pockets. "Mama-san was curious about what was happening with her girl." The two watched the girl disappear into the night.

"And?"

"I gave her some money for her trouble."

Michael grunted and turned toward the hotel. Bryce fell into step beside him. They were nearly back to their hotel when Bryce finally broke the silence. "You okay?"

"She probably wasn't any older than Marissa."

"Probably not."

"She should be playing with dolls."

"Or picking on her older brother's best friend."

Michael smiled, remembering the good-natured pranks his sisters used to pester good-natured Bryce. "Remember that first snow when April—"

"Yep."

"And the time you slept over and Marissa—"

"Don't remind me."

They walked on, each lost in his own thoughts. Stopping outside the hotel, Michael stared at the stars. "Think she'll do something better with her life?"

Bryce shrugged. "Well, I'd say that's up to her." He slapped Michael on the back. "But you gave her the option."

When personalizing your sidekick, ask yourself how the companion to your protagonist can

- Complete the hero's set of skills

- Provide contrast to the hero's style

- Balance the main character's personality

- Add humor or comedic relief

- Inadvertently solve the problem

- Speak the best dialog lines

- Behave loyally

- Personify the story's theme

Chapter Six

Adversaries, Antagonists And Other Villains

"Contains one of the best well-rounded villains I have read in a long time," reviewed Joseph Dyer about my book, *The Patent*.

This remains one of my favorite reviews because this reader recognized the multi-dimensions of the antagonist.

Story consists of three elements

- A character we care about

- The character's great need

- A great obstacle between the character we care about and their great need.

Frequently, the great obstacle is the antagonist, who can also be referred to as adversary, competitor, enemy, opponent, rival, or villain. Memorable antagonists include

- Claudius in *Hamlet*

- Darth Vader in *Star Wars*

- Fernand Mondego in *Count of Monte Cristo*

- Professor James Moriarty in *Sherlock Holmes*

- Sheriff of Nottingham in *Robin Hood*

- Voldemort in *Harry Potter*

Stories commonly feature a character line-up including protagonist, sidekick, antagonist, and mentor. In the same way a protagonist has flaws and weaknesses, an antagonist is not all bad.

Protagonists and Superheroes have flaws and weaknesses. In his youthful immaturity, Thor lost his father's trust. When possible, entwine the hero with the antagonist. Thor is at war with his brother. In the same way, the protagonist is not perfect, neither is an antagonist all bad. We kinda like Loki, at least as played by Tom Hiddleston.

Well-developed antagonists have a backstory. Once we realize the Wizard of Oz is as lost as Dorothy, we have insight into the motivation that drives his actions. In my novel, *The Patent*, Colonel Jai Yao is motivated by a desire to improve life for his countrymen.

While we see Yao threaten our hero, we are also privy to the choices he made to provide care for his frail parents. Like Javert in *Les Miserables*, Yao didn't set out to be evil on purpose. In the end, the reader and Yao are certain that even good motivations are no excuse for becoming a monster.

Story is conflict, and conflict is multi-dimensional. In addition to the friction between the hero and the antagonist, both characters are challenged by the tensions within their own personalities. In *Beauty and the Beast*, the Beast begins as the dangerous antagonist and transforms into Belle's happily ever after. That transformation is believable because the reader learns the reasons behind his circumstances and has sympathy for this character who is misunderstood, misjudged, and in a scenario he brought on himself through the common human traits of selfishness and pride.

Similarly, the Grinch begins as the evil protagonist of his own story, and experiences a character arc that ends with his transformation into a good character. Occasionally, as with Alex and *A Clockwork Orange*, the evil protagonist remains unredeemed. Antagonists can be human or inanimate including

- prejudice in *Pride and Prejudice*

- weather in *Chasing Sunrise*

- medical in *Wonder*

Suspense grows when the antagonist is a worthy opponent, and the opponent is worthy when we believe there is a good chance the protagonist will lose. For instance,

- in *The Sound of Music*, the German officer, backed by Hitler, is a worthy opponent to the Von Trapp family.

- Herod's cruelty made him a frightening opponent for Mary, Joseph, and baby Jesus.

- The British Empire proved to be a mighty opponent during the Revolution as George Washington's rag tag soldiers fought for liberty.

- Captain America fought Captain America – "I can do this all day." – when he went back in time to face himself in a desperate attempt to reverse the Thanos snap.

In *Moby Dick*, the adversarial great white whale does win in the end. Or is Captain Ahab the real villain in the story?

The clash between two opposing forces creates the narrative thread that spins into story. When two characters want the same single item, there can be only one

- Super Bowl trophy in the yearly play off

- husband for Belle in *Beauty and the Beast*

- one throne to rule the kingdom in Game of *Thrones*

- one ring of power in *Lord of the Rings*

- one owner of the litter of puppies *101 Dalmations*

Antagonists that vie against our character we care about can look like

- self: In Jack London's *Call of the Wild,* the hero wrestles himself for transformation

- God: *Jonah* attempts to weasel away from God's instructions

- destiny: *They Both Die at the End* lets readers know the destiny of each character

- character: *Three Musketeers* versus evil monarchs

- environment: Santiago in *The Old Man and the Sea*

- society or culture: Hester Prynne in *Scarlet Letter*

- machine: *2001 A Space Odyssey* pits characters against the artificial intelligence, HAL

- situation or circumstance: A schoolmaster develops a horse into the foundation of the Morgan breed in *Justin Morgan Had A Horse*

- the unknown: *Ender's Game* is leaders taking action without clear understanding of what they face

As you create an antagonist for your story, consider these questions.

What motivates the antagonist?

What is your antagonist most afraid of?

In what ways is your antagonist misjudged and misunderstood?

How does your antagonist bring out the best in your hero?

How does your antagonist bring out the worst in your hero?

How is your protagonist and antagonist connected?

What's the worst that can happen to the antagonist?

Chapter Seven

Mentors as Mirrors and Magnets

O f the four characters generally found in story – protagonist, sidekick, antagonist, and mentor – the role of a mentor gets its name from Homer's classic tale, *The Odyssey*, when the mentor actually has the name, Mentor. Disguised as the goddess of wisdom, Athena, Mentor instructs Telemachus to seek knowledge and stand against his enemies. Mentors have pretty much been dishing the same advice ever since.

"Use the force, Luke."
Obi-Wan Kenobi to Luke Skywalker in the first *Star Wars*

"If you're not enough without it, you'll never be enough with it."
Irving Blitzer to Derice Bannock in *Cool Runnings*

"Just a spoonful of sugar helps the medicine go down, in the most delightful way."

Mary Poppins to Jane and Michael Banks

The role of a mentor in story is to share knowledge and wisdom with the less experienced main character. According to author J.K. Rowling, Albus Dumbledore "has always had to be the one who knew, and who had the burden of knowing. And he would rather not know." As a mentor to the main character Harry Potter, "Dumbledore is a very wise man who knows that Harry is going to have to learn a few hard lessons to prepare him for what may be coming in his life."

Well-loved mentors include
- Obi-Wan Kenobi to Luke Skywalker

- Albus Dumbledore to the young scholar, Harry Potter

- Alfred Pennyworth to Batman

- M in Ian Fleming's James Bond series

- Mary Poppins to young Jane and Michael Banks

- Mr. Miyagi to the Karate Kid, Daniel LaRusso

- Haymitch Abernathy to Katniss Everdeen in *The Hunger Games*

- John Keating to his students in *Dead Poet's Society*

- Grandmother Tala to Moana

- Tony Stark's Ironman to Spiderman's Peter Parker

- Not all mentors are human

- Mufasa to Simba in *The Lion King*

- Mushu the Dragon to Mulan

- Jedi Master Yoda is another mentor to Luke Skywalker

- Jiminy Cricket to the puppet-turned-boy, Pinocchio

- Baloo the bear and Bagheera the panther to Mowgli in *Jungle Book*

Not all mentors are willing teachers. In these stories, the athlete wannabe grows in skills while the mentor experiences a transformative character arc.

- In the film, *Cool Runnings,* the Jamaican bobsled team invest a lot of time and effort convincing former Olympian bobsledder, Irving Blitzer to train them for the Olympics. Perhaps one of Irv's most insightful messages to team leader Derice Bannock was, "Getting what you want and being happy are two different things."

- Eddie the Eagle persistently works at his sport until Olympian jumper Bronson Peary agrees to be his coach.

- Secretariat's trainer, Lucian Laurin reluctantly agrees to prepare the horse to race.

In his *Save the Cat* series on writing, author Blake Snyder notes that the protagonist's dark night of the soul is frequently caused by the death of the main character's mentor. Without their mentor, the protagonist must carry on only to find they can do the right thing and be victorious without their mentor after all.

And while most mentors remain gone, there are exceptions. Obi-Wan becomes part of the force and occasionally gives the right reminders at the pertinent time.

In *Lord of the Rings*, Gandalf is overcome by the Balrog and falls for a long time before being burned by the Balrog's fire. Though darkness took Gandalf, and he passed away, as a divine spirit clothed in mortal form, the wizard returned to life some 20 days later. "Darkness took me," he described to Aragorn, Legolas, and Gimli in *The Two Towers*, "and I strayed out of thought and time, and I wandered far on roads that I will not tell." The experience changed the wizard from gray to white.

In C.S. Lewis' classic tale, *The Chronicles of Narnia*, Aslan is an iconic mentor to the about the Pevensie Children. The great, wise, and noble lion represents Christ, a reminder that for each of us, God provided a wise mentor in the Holy Spirit.

When adding a mentor to your story, consider these questions

- What must your main character do that he or she feels is impossible to accomplish?

- How can the mentor guide without rescuing?

- How will the mentor know the student is ready?

- Will the mentor leave the story partway through or be there to celebrate the main character's success?

- Is the mentor a willing or reluctant teacher?

- How will mentoring impact the mentor?

As you craft your characters, remember that mentors serve as mirrors for the protagonist's potential, and as a magnet drawing the main character toward their destiny.

Chapter Eight

How Well Do You Know Your Characters?

D o you know your character well enough to discern when they are lying?

The definition of character is the organization and structure of a person's character or personality. As the author – creator – of your story, the better you know your character the more three-dimensional the personality will be to your reader.

For instance, in Fyodor Dostoyevsky's 1866 novel, *Crime and Punishment*, Porfiry Petrovich is the head of the investigation department in charge of solving two murders. The Saint Petersburg detective encounters an innocent man who claims he committed the crime and a guilty man who denies he did the crime. The detective solves the mystery by knowing the deep aspects of the characters – what each is capable of and what each cannot do.

- Who is capable of lying and who is not?

- Who is capable of murder and who is not?

As an author, it is important to know your characters that well. Each character has their own backstory, settings and events that mold the interior and exterior of a person to be who they are. As Captain Jack Sparrow said in *Pirates of the Caribbean*, "The only rules that really matter are these: what a man can do and what a man can't do."

The more a writer knows the personality, background, and motivations about the character, the more compelling the story.

- Why is Indiana Jones afraid of snakes?

- Why is the Idumaean Herod so jealous for his throne as ruler of the Jews that he will kill babies?

- What happened in Jai Yao's childhood that makes him capable of kidnapping Marc Wayne in *The Patent*?

Make certain that actions and dialog align with each character's personality by doing an intake sheet for each character in the same fashion a counselor would do. This background information will prove valuable, providing insight into events that shaped what your character can do and what they cannot do.

Begin with the basics. What are the first influences that shaped your character?

Outward Appearance
Age
Sex

Height

Weight

Hair and eye color

Build

Way of moving

How does your character speak?

Beginning

About the character's beginning, was the birth planned, the child wanted, named for someone? Where did the character fall in the family birth order?

How old were the parents when the child was born? Did the mother experience good health? Was the birth easy or complicated? Did the child have good nutrition? Childhood diseases? What expectations did the parents have for their child? How prepared were the parents to be parents?

What socioeconomic status did the child grow up in? Were finances adequate, abundant, withheld, or lacking? Where and when did your character grow up? Culturally, what was happening in the child's circle, neighborhood, country, and world?

Early Life

While young, did the child experience the loss of significant people? Bond well or not with important people such as mother, father, siblings, extended family, neighbors, teachers, coaches? Did the family have pets? What scenarios impacted the child's ability to trust?

How well did the child learn? What education was available? Who were significant peers? Best friends? Mentors? What was the child's temperament toward others and self? What early life experiences made a lasting impact on the character?

For some, what the character can do and can't do will remain steady. For others, the story arc will provide the reader with believable reasons for your character to change what they can do and can't do.

Fill in the questions above to know what influences in your character's formative years made your character who they are when your reader first meets them.

Chapter Nine

What Did Your Character's Formative Years Form?

T he more a writer knows the personality, background, and motivations about a character, the more compelling the story. A story is a snapshot of a character's life, the noteworthy parts with the boring aspects conveniently trimmed away. Much about your character will not be included. But like a house that is built on a foundation not visible, the structure underneath determines a good deal about how the visible part responds to good and tough situations.

The same is true about character building. Each character has their own backstory, those unique settings and events that mold the interior and exterior of a person to be their own complex individual.

Last month we focused on the earliest foundation by asking questions about the character's beginnings. From the circumstances surrounding conception and birth until childhood begins to transition into adulthood, we did a deep dive into those formative childhood years. The next stage of personality development includes the middle and high school grades.

Some stories focus on the young adult season.

- How does *Harry Potter* discover who he is and come of age from childhood through high school graduation in an unfamiliar dimension?

- As a high schooler, can Bella Swan become someone different to love Edward Cullen in *Twilight*?

- The *Michael Vey* series features characters venturing through young adulthood fighting evil and learning to live with physical differences.

- C.S. Lewis set his young adult characters to learn about God through adventures in Narnia.

Here are three methods and questions to help you develop your character's backstory during those pivotal years after childhood.

1. Much like a psychologist, an author can ask probing questions that create a whole personality.

- When did puberty begin?

- Sexual awareness?

- Who was the character's first crush?

- First romance?

- What adults populated your character's world?

- Who were the parental surrogates such as coaches or teachers?

- As a teenager, when did your character separate from parents or from the place considered to be home?

- What was their first work experience?

- First job?

- What events contributed to the character's unique sense of self?

- How did unresolved issues from childhood impact the following years?

- What moods were typical?

- Was the character interested in learning or closeminded?

- What did education look like when your character was an early adult?

- When did a career come into play?

- Was there relocation?

- Separation from family?

- What hopes and dreams did your character harbor?

- What was accomplished?

- What frustrations or roadblocks prevented longed-for accomplishments?

- How did the character respond to culture?

- What habits were developed?

- Did the character experience sexual relationships, love relationships, or have children?

- Who were major influences during this period?

As an adult:
- What is your character's occupation and salary?

- Does the character practice faith?

- What type of people have become friends?

- Is family still involved?

- What hobbies, interests, and political views occupy their attention?

Whatever the age of your character in story, consider their inner appearance.

- What is your character afraid of?

- What is the worst thing that can happen?

- What have been the character's hardest emotions?

- Happiest?

- What triggers anger?

- When anger is triggered, how is that powerful emotion expressed?

- What does this character detest?

- Not understand?

- What is embarrassing?

- What is an inner-strength?

- How does the character receive and give love?

Perhaps most importantly:

- What does your character want most of all?

- What lies does the character believe?

- What secret does the character keep?

- How does the character see themself?

2) Another way to know your character is to interview them as you would for someone you are writing a feature article about.

What would you ask your character?

- How does your character answer the interview questions?

- What do you observe about your character?

- What are your character's actions, habits, behaviors?

- How does your character interact in their environment?

3) A third way to dive deeply into the person you are creating is to do a personality test for your character. There are a number of personality assessments online from the usual Myers-Briggs to the Enneagram.

Writing characters is a study on what people do and why they do it.

Once you know your character's background, rather than an information dump, drip this pertinent information about your character to the reader as needed for this story. Some information is only for the author to know the character well enough to write believably. Other information will be key for the reader to know ... eventually.

Chapter Ten

Surprise, Shock, and Delight Your Reader

R eaders like to be surprised. Characters that remain in our memories long after the story is complete often are the ones who in some way shocked, surprised, and delighted the reader.

In a romp of storytelling, the characters in *Fool's Gold* rapidly shift from enemies to partners to competitors to team players. The feature film starring Matthew McConaughey and Kate Hudson, is loosely based on the true story of treasure hunter Mel Fisher's discovery of the 1622 wreck of the *Nuestra Senora de Atocha*. The fun surprise is how character alliances break and form as new information comes to light, and in reaction to choices others make. Rather than casting characters into the customary roles of good guys versus bad guys, the writers rotate characters in and out of these places.

"Surprise the Broca," author James L. Rubart described. Named for the medical doctor and scientist who studied it in 1861, the Broca area of the brain is directly behind the prefrontal cortex. Everything we see and hear passes through Broca before arriving in the prefrontal area where we make decisions and choose to take action or not.

"Broca's area of the brain is like the filter or the bouncer of the brain," Rubart said. "It filters out information that's not surprising, provocative, or entertaining."

Memorable characters surprise, shock, and delight the Broca area of the reader's brain. The more a writer knows the personality, background, and motivations of a character, the greater the opportunity to highlight aspects to surprise the reader.

Page-turning stories include surprising, shocking, and delighting the reader through changing, disturbing, and heartwarming interactions between characters and settings, conflict and resolution.

Surprising changes such as

- The young man nicknamed Duchess vacillates between reasonable and unstable, valiant and injurious in Amor Towles' *The Lincoln Highway.*

- The illegitimate grandson of a lesser king is revealed to be the son of the High King Ambrosius Aurelianus in Mary Stewart's *Crystal Cave.* The author builds to a second striking revelation in *Hollow Hills* when Arthur learns he is not Merlin's illegitimate child, but the High King's heir.

- In Laura Montgomery's *Anne of Green Gables,* Anne shuns friendship with Gilbert, then discovers she loves him.

- Bucky is Steve Roger's best friend and support, then his

toughest enemy, and eventually redeemed team player in the Captain America / Avengers story.

Shocking such as

- The evil, heartless man bent on destroying others is brother to the brave, compassionate, mysterious rescuer, Bones, in Charles Martin's Murphy Shepherd series.

- The base evil done by those entrusted to do good in John Grisham's *A Time For Mercy*.

- The training practice that is actually the deciding war between Earth and an invader from space in Orson Scott Card's *Ender's Game*.

- Learning Katherine is Evelyn Mulwray's sister and daughter in Robert Towne's *Chinatown*.

- Delightful relationships including

- The complicated connections between an apartment complex full of unlikely residents in Fredrik Backman's *My Grandmother Says To Tell You She's Sorry*.

- A friendship formed between a spider and a runt pig in E.B. White's *Charlotte's Web*.

- A lost girl, a scarecrow, a lion, and a tinman in L. Frank Baum's *The Wonderful Wizard of Oz*.

- A U.S. Second Lieutenant on his first mission and a German ace in the middle of World War Two in. *A Higher Call* by Adam Makos.

"I didn't see that coming," frequently describes a reader's response when the author has woven in a surprising, shocking, and delightful characteristic, history, motivation, or behavior.

- Surprise your reader with unique experiences such as a HALO jump, diving the mile deep wall off the coast of St. Croix, and attending a social event in the center of the category 5 Hurricane Hugo in *Chasing Sunrise*.

- Shock your reader with information such as the impact of the Meissner Effect, the living conditions in poor villages, and the consequences of decisions on others in *The Patent*.

- Delight your reader with unusual settings such as working a shift in a satellite monitoring room, drinking from an ancient well deep in the Negev desert, and breakfasting on hummus, dates, and Turkish coffee at a Jewish kibbutz in *Secrecy Order*.

How can your characters surprise, shock, and delight your reader?

Chapter Eleven

What About Intimacy and Sex?

Intimacy and sex are part of life. These experiences have a profound impact on characters in story, often defining why a character does what they do. How does an author include sex in story?

J.R.R. Tolkien's *Lord of the Rings*, a masterful tale popular for generations, focuses on memorable characters in a multi-level plot, experiencing sensational settings and speaking quotable dialog.

On film, the story takes place over six full-length feature movies. In book and film, there is no profanity and no sex scenes.

- *The Lord of the Rings: The Fellowship of the Ring* (2001)

- *The Lord of the Rings: The Two Towers* (2002)

- *The Lord of the Rings: Return of the King* (2003)

- *The Hobbit: An Unexpected Journey* (2012)

- *The Hobbit: The Desolation of Smaug* (2013)

- *The Hobbit: The Battle of the Five Armies* (2014)

The original manuscripts, totaling 9,250 pages and preserved in the J. R. R. Tolkien Collection at Wisconsin's Marquette University, were initially published in three volumes. Tolkien considered his work a heroic romance.

Tolkien's Aragorn and Arwen remain true to one another despite separations caused by the oppressive threat of the growing power of Sauron. Their moments together are beautifully romantic, penned in a fashion that children can read. In the final film, Aragorn and Arwen are reunited as Aragorn takes his place as king. In a sweet and very public moment, as their faces almost touch, we know they will spend the rest of their lives together.

In story, as in life, intimacy shows up in many forms from friendship to romantic relationships to events completely unloving.

Explicit scenes and erotica have an audience. There are readers looking for such content. Authors who tell a story and include romance and encounters in a wholesome fashion have a broader audience as the story is appropriate to younger ages and to those who prefer to focus on plot and character development while allowing the character's bedroom to remain private.

In the film, *Gone With The Wind*, Rhett Butler carries his wife, Scarlett O'Hara, up the curving staircase.

Similarly, at the end of *Chasing Sunrise*, Michael Northington lifts his bride into his arms and carries her into their future.

Sometimes the sexual encounter is far from romantic.

The Chosen portrayed this well in Season 1, Episode 1 when a Roman soldier brutalizes Mary Magdalene. Pushing her onto the bed, as his shadow falls across her face, the scene ends. The viewer is aware of what happened without needing details.

In Khaled Hosseini's *The Kite Runner*, the protagonist gives a brief view of a bully overpowering a boy. The protagonist turns away yet the reader understands how the violence imprints on both the protagonist and the victim. Later, we learn the unexplained treatment of the two boys by the father is because the boys are half-brothers.

The Slave Across the Street is the riveting true story of an upscale Detroit teenager trafficked for two years. We wanted the book to provide awareness to youth who are targeted, and to those who work with children and teens. The reader accompanies Theresa as she is taken into a room with men waiting. Then the scene ends. There is no reason to describe anything more.

As a writer, where can you creatively show intimacy and allude to sex while staying family-friendly to reach a wider audience?

World's End of the *Pirates of the Caribbean* film series wraps up with Elizabeth Swann wearing one of Will Turner's boots. In the two-and-a-half-minute beach scene, the viewer understands that after three movies packed with action, adventure, and seemingly impossible odds that kept the two apart, the married lovers have at last spent a single day together.

When penning intimacy and sex in a story, consider your goals.

- Who is your audience?

- What is your genre?

- What is your reader trusting you to write?

- Is sex critical to the story?

- Is the scene more powerful when hinted at, alluded to, or done off-stage?

- How can you best tell the story in a way that best honors the tale, your reader, and yourself as an author?

Chapter Twelve

Crafting Creative Characters

Writers come in many types. Traditionally, authors work mostly as outliners, plotters, or plungers, while there are hybrids of these. While I lean to plunger, each project has its own requirements. Characters created in a historical timeline require careful planning which looks a lot like an outline.

Outliner

JK Rowling created main character, Harry Potter, with winsome characteristics including eyeglasses, curiosity, and a deep longing for family and belonging. She gave him a quest to defeat Lord Voldemort, fueled by his parents' murders. Great characters are driven by a deep-seated motivation and have a goal they are trying to reach.

In *Chasing Sunrise*, Michael Northington grew up in a single-parent home. He longs for adventure and to make his life count by being part of a military that shows up when someone calls 9-1-1.

Plotter

Bill Myers, whose books and films sold more than eight million copies and won more than 60 national and international awards, knows where his story will go from beginning to end before he puts words on his manuscript. The author of numerous series for kids, teens, and adults, likes to use the bubble diagram technique. He described writing a seed idea onto a yellow legal pad and circling the idea. From there, Bill creates a bubble diagram, listing a variety of *what next* possibilities, followed by another level of potential plot points, and then another and another until the legal pad is filled.

With a highlighter, Myers reviews the original idea, and marks the best next event in each sequence. With this method, he maps the entirety of the story. His writing process involves following the highlighted trail on the legal pad from chapter one until 'The End.'

Bill crafts characters that are awkward, outside the popular crowd, imaginative, and friends with others who are socially inept. His characters resonate, touching on those guarded places where readers have also felt they don't fit in.

Plunger

My tendency is to be a plunger. *Chasing Sunrise* began as a scene that hung around my thoughts. I wrote the picture, expecting this would be a chapter in the center of the story. In the end, that first scene turned out to be the final chapter. Who knew?!

As a verbal processor, I usually don't know what I'm thinking until it comes out my mouth. Similarly, sitting at my laptop, Mac(Beth), parts of the story flow as fresh to me as they will be to the reader. Because the scenes do not appear in sequence, I write the scenes formulating in my brain. Ideas that show up later frequently reveal information that fills in earlier gaps. "No wonder the bad guy behaves in that way." When the manuscript is nearly complete, I rearrange chapters as needed for the story to make sense, add transitions, and fill in details.

Linear

Estee Zandee writes her novels sequentially from beginning to end. Taking a break once, she returned to her manuscript to discover "what the bad guy was doing while I was away." Her natural creative process is more linear.

Hybrids

Some projects organically require an author to employ a different method than their natural go-to. There is no right or wrong way to plot a story. Write your story and the characters who populate your plot using the method that works for you to get the story done, or using the method the project requires to be accurate, believable, and complete.

Chapter Thirteen

Thank You

Thank you for reading *Creative Characters* by P.S. Wells (PeggySue Wells) in the Quick Guide to Writing Well series *Creative Characters* is available in ebook and paperback.

If you have a moment, please leave a review on your favorite bookseller website. Reviews are the best gift you give an author.

Titles you may like by P.S. Wells include:

Quick Guides to Writing Well series
Pivotal Plots
Sensational Settings
Creative Characters
Dynamic Dialog
Point of View

Marc Wayne Adventure series
Chasing Sunrise

Check out the audio version of *Chasing Sunrise* read by Scott Hoke

The Patent

Secrecy Order

Unnatural Cause

Homeless for the Holidays

Check out the audio version of *Homeless for the Holidays* read by voice actor Katie Leigh

Personal Growth titles

The Ten Best Decisions A Single Mom Can Make

Slavery in the Land of the Free

The Girl Who Wore Freedom

C heck out these titles by PS Wells and PeggySue Wells

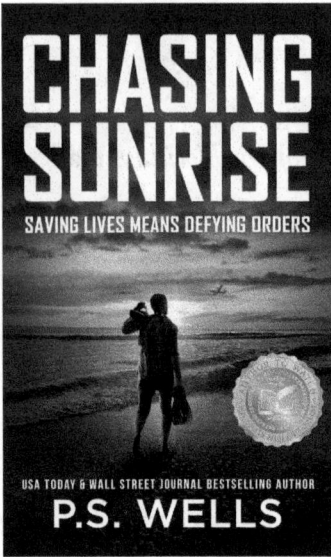

When an assignment results in a friend's death, Michael Northington seeks solace on St. Croix. When deadly players blow into St. Croix at the same time Hurricane Hugo unleashes its fury, will Michael's skills be enough to protect those he loves?

Also available in audio version, narrated by Scott Hoke.

When the world teeters on the verge of World War III, the nation that develops a patent attorney's invention will be militarily invincible in the race for global dominance. Now America's enemies have stolen the plans and kidnapped the inventor. Marc Wayne must find a way of escape before his captors realize the invention is theoretical. Or is it?

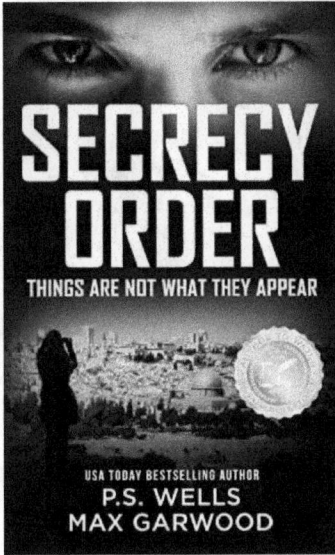

Powerful nations hunt for Marc Wayne and his invention which promises to redefine weapons and global warfare. Meanwhile, in a remote hiding place, Marc serves as bait in hopes to turn his predators into prey. When an illegal arms dealer leverages Marc for his own ends, will Marc ever see home and family again? As time runs out, can he trust the electro-physicist, Lei Quong, enough to escape with her?

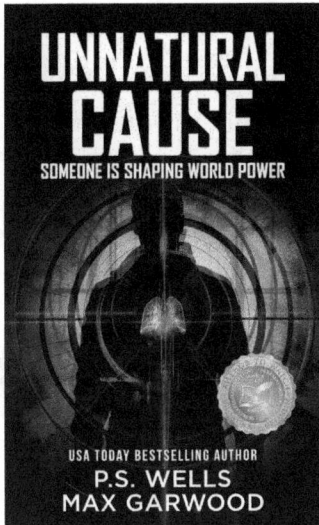

Winner of the best mystery suspense of the year, *Unnatural Cause* unpacks long unsolved family mysteries. Using a device that creates a deadly embolism from a remote location, someone is targeting world leaders to shape world power. But when Marc Wayne stops those who wield the ability to commit consequence-free murder, he finds he has played right into the mastermind's plans.

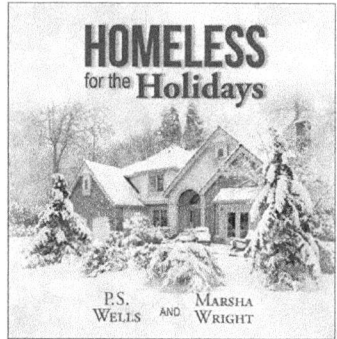

Christmas is coming, and Jack Baker's finances, friends, and future are as gone as last year's holiday. Amidst the holiday traditions and trappings, one family learns what is truly important when they lose all they have, and find they still have everything.

Also available in audio version read by voice actor Katie Leigh.

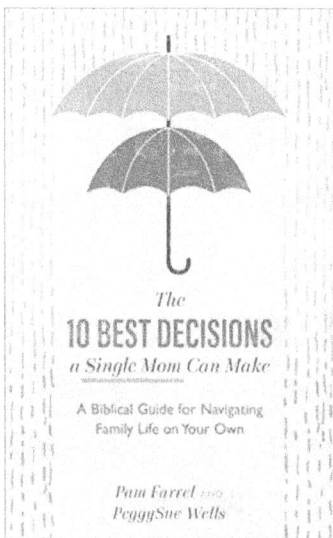

No matter how you became a single mom, you share the same challenges and fears all single moms have. How are you going to do this on your own? With humor, and sage advice, PeggySue Wells (single parent of seven children) provides practical helps and tangible tips to help you succeed.

A clear picture of how human trafficking happens and how prevalent it is today. We ended slavery once before in the United States, and we can do it again.

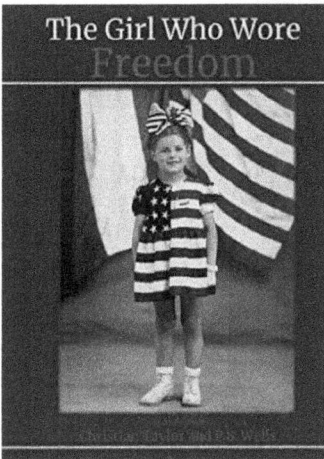

SLAVERY IN THE LAND OF THE FREE

A STUDENT'S GUIDE TO MODERN DAY SLAVERY

THERESA FLORES
PEGGYSUE WELLS

The Girl Who Wore Freedom

On June 6, 1944, when Dany was five years old, U.S. soldiers liberated her village from Nazi control. Soldiers established a base on Utah Beach near Dany's home, shared their provisions, and befriended the people of Sainte Marie du Mont. From the parachutes of the American soldiers who freed her, Dany's mother sewed a red, white, and blue dress resembling the American flag. Dany wore the dress at the yearly D-Day celebration and became known as *The Girl Who Wore Freedom*.

PeggySue's Particulars
to Pen

POINT OF VIEW

A Quick Guide to
Writing Well

PEGGYSUE WELLS

You want to write and write well. Point of view is the writer's most powerful tool to elicit emotion in the reader. POV can make the difference between a character appearing as a killer or a king. Learn how to pen the proper POV that compels a reader to turn pages until reaching the end.

You want to write and write well. Use this quick guide to amplify, intensify, and magnify through plot to craft a compelling story.

In this quick how-to guide, learn the particulars to craft pivotal plots that create compelling stories.

PeggySue's Particulars
to Pen

PIVOTAL PLOTS

A Quick Guide To
Writing Well

PEGGYSUE WELLS

Peggy Sue's Particulars
to Pen

**CREATIVE
CHARACTERS**

A Quick Guide To
Writing Well

PEGGYSUE WELLS

You want to write and write well. Use this quick guide to craft creative characters that live in the reader's mind beyond the final page of a story.

Three essentials are common to every compelling story.

1) a character the reader cares about

2) a very great life-changing, world-impacting need the character must achieve

3) a great obstacle between the character we care about and the character's life-changing, world-impacting need.

In Creative Characters, learn how to craft characters who are believable, three-dimensional, and remain in the reader's memory long after the book is read.

Stories happen in a place and that place is the setting. Settings come in four personalities.

The personalities types of setting are

- Passive

- Active

- Like a Character

- Is the Story

PeggySue's Particulars to Pen

SENSATIONAL
SETTINGS

A Quick Guide To
Writing Well

PEGGYSUE WELLS

What does the setting sound like, feel like, and look like? If you plan to write a book or want to improve a story, place the tale in a sensational setting. Sensational Settings: A Quick Guide to Writing Well shows you how.

PeggySue's Particulars
to Pen

DYNAMIC DIALOG

A Quick Guide To
Writing Well

PEGGYSUE WELLS

Dialog is what characters say. Powerful stories are dialog-driven through carefully chosen word selections. The four purposes of dialog in your story include:

1. Move your story forward

2. Reveal something important about your plot

3. Show something important about your character

4. Give your character a unique voice

Conversations that take place between characters are often the reader's favorite part. Add value to your story by writing dialog that is clever, creative, and concise.

About the Author

P.S. Wells is a USA Today and Wall Street Journal bestselling author of 35 books (so far). When not writing, Wells rides horses, parasails, scuba dives, and skydives. She is the founder of SingleMomCircle.com

Connect with P.S. Wells at PeggySueWells.com

www.ingramcontent.com/pod-product-compliance
Lightning Source LLC
Chambersburg PA
CBHW060519280326
41933CB00014B/3028